Contents

Introduction

The following leaders have been selected as the Top Ten from hundreds of leaders that have undoubtedly changed our world. Why have these ten made it and not others?

✱ Firstly, we've left out religious leaders in order not to offend anybody!

Religious leaders like Buddha are not included in the list.

Famous leaders from the past, like Cleopatra (shown here welcoming Caesar), were important in their day, but have not affected the modern world.

✱ Secondly, the leader must have affected or inspired the world, not just a part of it (whether for good or bad).

THE TOP TEN
LEADERS
THAT CHANGED THE WORLD

Anita Ganeri

W
FRANKLIN WATTS
LONDON•SYDNEY

This edition published in the UK in 2011 by Franklin Watts

Franklin Watts
338 Euston Road
London NW1 3BH

Franklin Watts Australia
Level 17/207 Kent Street
Sydney, NSW 2000

A CIP catalogue record for this book is available from the British Library.

Dewey Classification: 920'.02

ISBN 978 1 4451 0645 8

Franklin Watts is a division of Hachette Children's Books, an Hachette UK company.
www.hachette.co.uk

THE TOP TEN LEADERS THAT CHANGED THE WORLD
was produced for Franklin Watts by
David West Children's Books, 7 Princeton Court, 55 Felsham Road, London SW15 1AZ

Copyright © 2009 David West ☷ Children's Books

Designer and illustrator: David West
Editor: Katharine Pethick

Photographic credits:
19bl, eurok; 19br, jiashiang; 22tl, p_c_w; 23tl, Paul Mannixj

Printed in China

✱ Thirdly, the effects of their leadership must still be felt today.

You might disagree with the people that have been chosen. In which case you might like to put together your own list.

Alexander the Great conquered a vast empire but his influence was felt most strongly around the Mediterranean and in the Middle East.

Julius Caesar (100 BC – 44 BC)

Julius Caesar was born in Rome at a time when rival Roman armies were fighting for power. He was part of an influential political family, and left Rome in 82 BC in fear of his life. He returned in 73 BC and entered politics. Caesar spent two years as governor of Spain (then a Roman province), and then became governor of Gaul (in modern-day France). He stayed in Gaul for nearly ten years, leading military campaigns. In 53 BC, Pompey became leader of the Senate. He feared Caesar's power and ordered Caesar to return to Rome. Caesar refused.

In 49 BC, with a legion of loyal soldiers, Caesar crossed the River Rubicon, which marked the northern boundary of Italy, triggering a civil war. Then Caesar's army marched south towards Rome.

Rome's territories 44 BC

Roman Empire 3rd century AD

The map shows how, following Caesar's conquests, Rome expanded to dominate Europe and the Middle East lasting until the 5th century AD.

Caesar accepts the surrender of Gaulish leader Vercingetorix. The conquest of Gaul made Caesar very powerful.

MASTER OF ROME

Within a few months, Caesar had control of Italy but it took him four years to defeat Pompey and subdue all the far-flung Roman provinces. Caesar finally returned to Rome in 45 BC and was made dictator for life. He made improvements to the unfair tax system, the legal system and the Senate, and settled Rome's appalling debts. However, Rome was a republic, run by the people, and some senators thought Caesar was becoming too powerful. They hatched a plot to kill him and Caesar was assassinated in March 44 BC. To be a success in Ancient Rome required both political and military skill. Caesar was a brilliant speaker in the Roman Senate and a master tactician on the battlefield.

Apart from being a great leader, admired across the world, Caesar is also remembered for his reform of the calendar, known as the Julian calendar, a legacy that lasts to the present day.

Emperors of the German Empire were called Kaiser, after Caesar's name.

The Julian calendar remained in use into the 20th century in some countries as a national calendar, but it has generally been replaced by the modern Gregorian calendar.

Elizabeth I (1533 – 1603)

'I know I have the body of a weak and feeble woman; but I have the heart and stomach of a king.' So said Queen Elizabeth I in 1588, as she rallied troops gathered to fight off an imminent Spanish invasion. The daughter of Henry VIII of England and his second wife, Anne Boleyn, Elizabeth was raised as a Protestant, at a time when Protestants and Catholics were at war with each other. During the reign of her Catholic half-sister Mary, she was put under house arrest for many years. On Mary's death in 1558, the Protestant Elizabeth became queen. In 1588, Philip of Spain sent a huge fleet of ships – the Armada – to destroy the English navy and put a Catholic ruler on the throne. But the invasion never arrived. Unbeknown to Elizabeth and her army, the Armada had already been routed.

GOOD QUEEN BESS

The defeat of the Spanish Armada was followed by celebrations throughout England. The victory confirmed Elizabeth's popularity with her people, who called her by her nickname, Good Queen Bess. Elizabeth proved to be a wise leader. She relied on a group of important advisors called the Privy Council but used her own judgement of character to manage

Under Elizabeth, England became an important Protestant nation in Europe for the first time.

the rivalry between the powerful English aristocrats. Elizabeth also encouraged her seafaring adventurers, such as Drake and Raleigh, to explore and raid Spanish treasure ships to fill the country's coffers.

Raleigh's settlement at Roanoke Island in North America ended in failure but paved the way for later colonies. In 1600, Elizabeth granted a Royal charter to the East India Company, which ended up trading with China and India. **These were the beginnings of a British Empire that would change the world for centuries to come.**

This period in history saw a huge leap in exploration. Elizabeth encouraged explorers like Sir Francis Drake who managed to circumnavigate the globe.

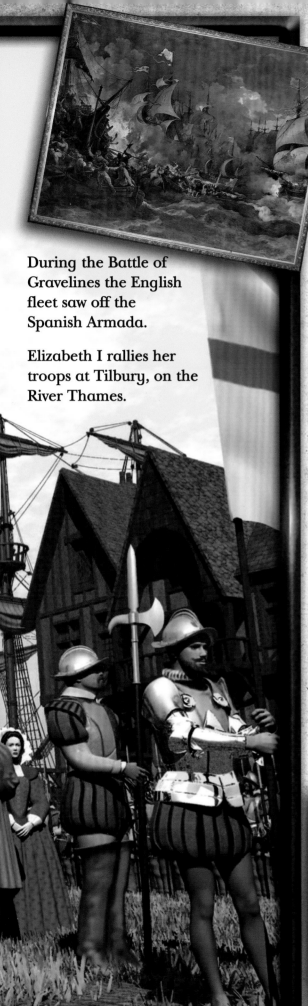

During the Battle of Gravelines the English fleet saw off the Spanish Armada.

Elizabeth I rallies her troops at Tilbury, on the River Thames.

George Washington (1732 – 1799)

On Christmas night 1776, George Washington led his troops of the Continental Army across the icy Delaware River in New Jersey, USA to launch a surprise attack on British forces at Trenton. It was just one of the victories for the Continental Army during the American War of Independence. Washington was born into a rich farming family in the British colony of Virginia. In his 20s, he gained valuable military experience in the Seven Years War against French colonists. In the 1770s, disagreements between the colonists and the British government over unfair taxes led to the American War of Independence, which began in 1775. By then, Washington had become a leading political figure and was made Commander-in-Chief of the colonial military forces. He formed the Continental Army and prepared to fight for independence.

AMERICAN INDEPENDENCE

Washington oversees his farm at Mount Vernon, Virginia.

A US coin featuring Washington.

In 1776, the colonists declared independence, creating the United States of America. Washington's Continental Army gradually gained the upper hand, finally winning the war at the Battle of Yorktown, in 1781. Washington resigned and returned to his Virginia farm. But he was persuaded to lead the writing of the United States Constitution in 1787 and, in 1789, was elected the first President of the United States of America. He was re-elected in 1792 and served until 1797. Then he finally retired to his farm, where he died two years later. **Washington, the most famous founding father, led the Americans from a collection of colonies to a new, independent nation that has become the superpower we know today.**

George Washington resigns his commission.

Washington is commemorated in street and building names all across America, including The Washington Monument – the world's tallest obelisk.

Napoleon (1769 – 1821)

In October 1795, during the French Revolution, troops loyal to the royal family marched into Paris, aiming to regain control of France from the republican government. A young general, Napoleon Bonaparte, took command of the republican forces, who were seriously outnumbered. Using brilliant leadership, Napleon stopped the royalists in their tracks. This small but decisive battle became known as 13 Vendemiaire (after its date in the French Revolutionary calendar). It saved the republican government and made Napoleon a hero. Napoleon had joined the army as an artillery officer at the age of 16, and had risen quickly through the ranks. His first military success was a victory over French anti-republican and British forces at Toulon in 1793.

By 1796, he had control of the French army in Italy. Over the next few years, he led victories for France over Austria, and conquered Egypt.

EMPEROR OF FRANCE

Bonaparte made himself Emperor Napoleon I of France at his coronation in Notre Dame, in Paris.

The Battle of 13 Vendemiaire (5 October 1795) saw Napoleon victorious against Royalist troops.

In 1799, Napoleon returned to France from Egypt, overthrew the government, and took charge. Five years later, he was created Emperor of France, and set about expanding the French empire with military campaigns in eastern Europe, Spain and Italy. At home, he changed the French laws to give the people better rights. (These were known as the 'Napoleonic Code'.) But after a failed attempt to invade Russia in 1812, the empire collapsed. Napoleon was exiled to the island of Elba but managed to escape and seize power again. Amongst others, Britain, Austria and Prussia decided to invade France to stop him. Napoleon led an army to face them but was defeated at the Battle of Waterloo, in Belgium. Again, he was exiled, this time to the remote island of St Helena in the Atlantic Ocean. He died there six years later.

A British cartoon showing Napoleon being exiled to Elba.

The 1815 Battle of Waterloo was a disaster for Napoleon.

Napoleon's lasting fame is as a military genius but his legacy also includes the Napoleonic Code. With its stress on clearly written and accessible law, it has strongly influenced laws around the world.

13

Joseph Stalin (1878 – 1953)

In 1894, a teenage Joseph Stalin began studies at theological college. But theology fell by the wayside when he heard about the political ideas of German philosopher Karl Marx from his fellow students. Stalin decided to support the revolution against the Russian monarchy and joined a communist group called the Bolsheviks. He organised bank robberies, kidnappings and other illegal activities to raise money for the group. Several times, Stalin was arrested, imprisoned and exiled to Siberia but he quickly became a respected figure in the Bolshevik movement. In 1917, the Russian Revolution began. The Russian monarchy was overthrown and Stalin was released from prison. After a civil war, the Bolsheviks took power and, in 1922, the Soviet Union was formed. The same year Stalin was elected as general secretary of the Communist Party. From this extremely powerful position Stalin cleverly eliminated his political opponents to become outright leader of the Soviet Union.

RUTHLESS TACTICS

Stalin was deeply suspicious of his political rivals and ruthlessly eliminated them. Millions were executed or sent to labour camps, in a reign of terror known as the Great Purge. In 1941, Hitler launched an invasion of

Armed Bolsheviks take aim in the revolution of 1917.

Stalin whips up support for the Bolsheviks at a political rally.

Russia's soldiers answer Stalin's call to defend the city that bears his name – Stalingrad in 1942.

the Soviet Union. Rallied by Stalin, the Red Army eventually drove the Germans back, but at the cost of tens of millions of lives. When Germany was defeated in 1945, the Soviets controlled most of eastern Europe. To keep a firm grip on power, Stalin made sure his neighbouring countries were run by

'The big three' – Churchill, Roosevelt, and Stalin meet in 1945 to decide the future of Europe.

communist governments. Stalin was a ruthless leader and often used brutal methods. **But under his leadership, the Soviet Union emerged as an industrial and military power that dominated eastern Europe. After his death he was denounced, beginning the period known as de-Stalinization.**

Ruthless and determined, Stalin was a powerful personality and leader.

15

Adolf Hitler (1889 – 1945)

In 1939, German leader Adolf Hitler invaded Poland and World War
II began. Germany soon had control over most of Europe and in 1941, as part
of his plan for world domination, Hitler ordered an attack on Russia. Born in
Austria, Hitler fought for Germany in World War I and was decorated for
bravery. In 1920 he joined the National Socialist German Workers' Party
(the Nazis), aiming to regain Germany's power after its defeat in World War
I. The party was also fiercely anti-Jewish and anti-communist. In 1921, the
charismatic Hitler became party leader, increasing the party's popularity.
In 1933, as German chancellor, he quickly took total control, making himself
dictator. Soon he was ready to put his master plan into action.

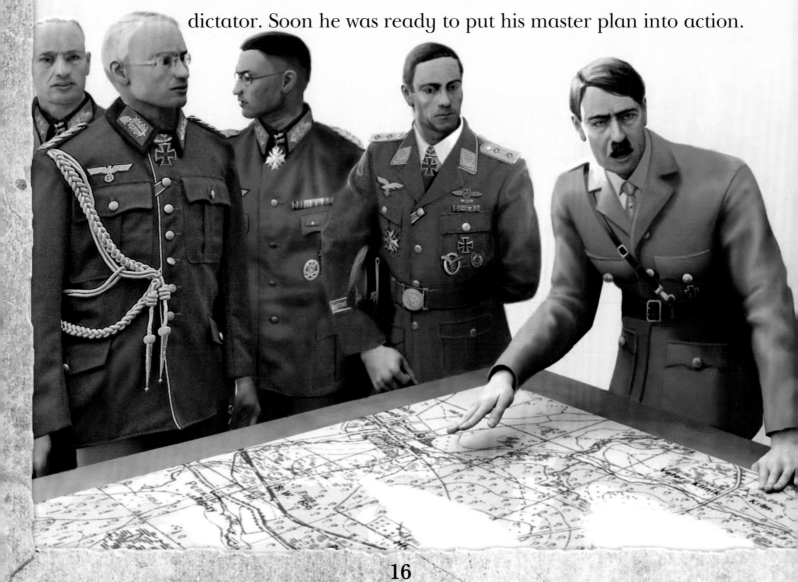

Hitler speaks in the Reichstag (German parliament) in 1941. His rise to the top took just 13 years.

Hitler's domination of Europe did not last, and by 1945 his forces were in retreat. As the Soviet Red Army reached the outskirts of Berlin, Hitler committed suicide. But his forces had committed appalling acts before and during the war, killing millions of people considered by Hitler to be inferior, including an estimated six million Jews. At the end of World War II, the political map of Europe changed radically. Germany was divided in two, and so was Europe. The Soviets occupied the east and the other Allies, including USA and Britain, occupied the west. This situation eventually led to the Cold War. **Hitler was responsible for plunging the entire globe into a war which, when over, resulted in a world divided into East and West.**

Auschwitz extermination camp

Modern day Neo-Nazis – another of Hitler's legacies

HITLER DEAD

Fuehrer Fell at CP, German Radio Says; Doenitz at Helm, Vows War Will Continue

Hemmed in by Allied and Russian forces, Hitler took his own life.

Mao Zedong (1893 – 1976)

Mao Zedong became interested in Communism whilst working at Beijing University in 1918. In 1921, he visited Shanghai, where he helped start the Chinese Communist Party. The Party's aim was a revolution against traditional Chinese society, transferring power to the peasants. Six years later, the Kuomintang, the Communists' rivals, seized power and civil war broke out. Forced south into a region called Jiangxi, the Communists later set up their own government, with Mao as its leader. Mao gradually built up an army, known as the Red Army. In 1933, the Kuomintang attacked and pushed the Red Army to the brink of defeat.

To escape, Mao led the Red Army on a 9,600-kilometre journey north to safety. Known as the Long March, it was a treacherous journey – of the 100,000 who set out, just 20,000 arrived at the end.

Mao fought in the revolution of 1911 that toppled the last Emperor of China.

Mao greets US President Richard Nixon in 1972.

CULTURAL REVOLUTION

After World War II, civil war broke out again in China. This time the Communists gradually got the upper hand and, in 1949, the People's Republic of China was founded, with Mao as its chairman. Now Mao could start his revolution in earnest. He improved schools and health care, built new roads and power plants, confiscated farms from landlords and gave them to the peasants. In 1958, Mao planned his 'Great Leap Forward', ordering rural communities to grow all their own food. But the plan failed badly. Millions of Chinese died in famines and, in 1959, Mao resigned. He returned to power in 1966 to launch the Cultural Revolution. This challenged anybody, especially intellectuals, who disagreed with his ideas. Mao remained president until his death in 1976. **By founding the People's Republic of China, Mao paved the way for the country to become the superpower it is today.**

Mao idolised with Joseph Stalin on a Soviet poster

The *Sayings of Chairman Mao*, also known as *The Little Red Book*.

Mao's influence is like that of Qin, the Emperor who unifed China in the 3rd century BC (see page 26).

Mohandas Gandhi (1869 – 1948)

When Mohandas Gandhi was born in 1869, India, which included Pakistan and Bangladesh, was part of the British Empire. After studying in London, Gandhi practised law in South Africa. He was appalled at the way Indian workers were treated and encouraged non-violent protest, which he called 'satyagraha' or 'force of truth'. In 1915, Gandhi returned to India and, from 1919, led the Indian campaign for independence from Britain, boycotting British goods and refusing to co-operate with the authorities. In 1930, only the British could make and sell salt, a vital part of the Indian diet. In protest, Gandhi led a 'Salt March' to the sea, resulting in a change to the law.

FORCE OF TRUTH

In 1944, the British agreed to grant India independence. Many Indian Muslims wanted a separate country for themselves, leaving India for the majority Hindus. Gandhi was against this as he thought all Indians, regardless of religion, should be able to live together. In 1947, India finally became independent, but parts of it were divided off to create Muslim

Gandhi as a young lawyer in South Africa in 1900.

Pakistan. Partition, as this division was called, caused violent riots during which hundreds of thousands of people were displaced or died. Deeply distressed, Gandhi began a series of fasts to the death that eventually stopped the fighting. In 1948, Gandhi was assassinated by a Hindu extremist. **His use of non-violent protest helped lead India to independence and made him an influential figure to other protest leaders such as Martin Luther King and Nelson Mandela.**

The Partition of India led to the mass relocation of Hindu and Muslim Indians.

Gandhi fasting in 1924. Ghandi used fasting as a political weapon in the 1940s.

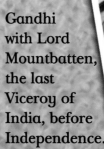

Gandhi with Lord Mountbatten, the last Viceroy of India, before Independence.

Martin Luther King (1929 – 1968)

'I have a dream,' proclaimed Martin Luther King, 'that my four little children will one day live in a nation where they will not be judged by the colour of their skin but by the content of their character.' These words were part of King's famous speech at a civil-rights demonstration in Washington, DC, USA in 1963. At that time in the USA, there was still racial segregation in some states, and black and white people were not allowed to mix. An African-American, King became a clergyman in 1954. In 1955, he led a successful bus boycott in the town of Montgomery, where black people were forced to sit at the back of buses. Many more non-violent protests followed. The protestors were often attacked by white extremists and King's home was bombed. Often King and the protestors were arrested.

THE DREAM FULFILLED

Under Martin Luther King's leadership, the civil rights movement finally got results. Segregation ended in the city of Birmingham, Alabama, in 1963, after police attacked protestors with fire hoses and dogs. The Civil Rights Act of 1964 outlawed segregation and racial discrimination and, in the same year, Martin Luther King was awarded the Nobel Peace Prize.

King continued to protest for voting rights and better conditions for black people. Then, in 1968, tragedy struck when King was assassinated in Memphis, Tennessee.

By helping to gain equal rights for African-Americans, and showing that injustices could be righted by non-violent protest, Martin Luther King deserves to be regarded as one of the top ten leaders who changed the world.

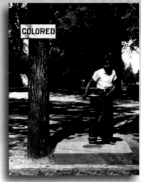

A segregated drinking fountain in North Carolina, USA, in the 1930s

The Washington march was a monumental event.

White Americans protest against mixed-race schools in 1959.

King's achievements have inspired 21st century leaders like US President Barack Obama.

23

Nelson Mandela (BORN 1918)

In 1948, the white National Party came to power in Africa. It introduced a system of unfair laws, known as apartheid, which forced black people and other minorities to live apart from whites, and banned them from important jobs. It also introduced new 'pass laws', forcing black people to carry identity papers at all times. Lawyer Nelson Mandela was a member of the African National Congress (ANC), which campaigned for civil rights for black people. In 1952, Mandela became ANC deputy president and took part in non-violent demonstrations against apartheid. In 1960, during protests against the pass laws, 69 demonstrators were killed by the police. Reluctantly, Mandela set up an armed section of the ANC that carried out acts of sabotage against the government.

In 1962, Mandela was arrested, convicted of treason and sentenced to life in prison.

Mandela's prison cell on Robben Island. Below, Mandela sits and sews prison clothes in the yard of Robben Island prison.

RAINBOW NATION

From prison, Mandela secretly kept in contact with his ANC colleagues and wrote most of his autobiography. He remained the figurehead of the anti-apartheid movement. During the 1980s, international pressure grew on South Africa to free Mandela. He was finally released in 1990, after 27 years in prison, and became leader of the ANC. With South African president, F. W. de Klerk, he negotiated the end of apartheid and was jointly awarded the Nobel Peace Prize. After the country's first free elections in 1994, Mandela was sworn in as President of South Africa. He remained President until 1999. **More than anyone else, Mandela helped to lead South Africa from being a racist country to a multi-racial democracy, and is seen as an influential leader in the fight for racial equality throughout the world.**

FOR USE BY WHITE PERSONS

THESE PUBLIC PREMISES AND THE AMENITIES THEREOF HAVE BEEN RESERVED FOR THE EXCLUSIVE USE OF WHITE PERSONS.

By Order Provincial Secretary

VIR GEBRUIK DEUR BLANKES

HIERDIE OPENBARE PERSEEL EN DIE GERIEWE DAARVAN IS VIR DIE UITSLUITLIKE GEBRUIK VAN BLANKES AANGEWYS.

Op Las Provinsiale Sekretaris

An apartheid sign

A 1986 concert campaigning to free Nelson Mandela.

Mandela with US President Bill Clinton in 1993, one year before he became president of South Africa.

25

The Best of the Rest

EMPEROR QIN (259 – 210 BC)

In 221 BC, Qin Shi Huangdi, ruler of the Qin Dynasty, proclaimed himself the first emperor of China and gave his name to the country. A powerful and ruthless ruler, Qin abolished the system of local states and established a strong, central government. He also standardised the country's script, laws, currency, and weights and measures. Until then, each state had had its own systems which had been very confusing.

Qin also ordered the building of the Great Wall of China, to keep out hostile invaders from the north. The emperor died in 210 BC, aged just 49. His extraordinary tomb was guarded by an army of thousands of life-sized clay warriors – the Terracotta Army – which was rediscovered in 1974.

The famous Terracotta Army was built to guard Qin's tomb.

GENGHIS KHAN (ca 1162 – 1227)

A brilliant soldier and politician, Genghis Khan was a Mongol leader whose armies conquered the largest land empire in history. The Mongols were nomadic horsemen from Mongolia who were originally split into warring tribes. On the death of his father, Genghis, then named Temuchin, became chief of one of the tribes at the age of 13. Showing great leadership, he soon began to build a powerful army to gain control over his neighbours. By 1206, he had become ruler of Mongolia and was given the title Genghis Khan, meaning 'universal ruler'.

His armies then swept through Central Asia, ruthlessly killing anyone who blocked their path. In 1225, Genghis proceeded with his conquest of China, completed after his death by his grandson, Kublai Khan.

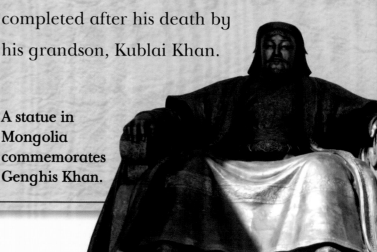

A statue in Mongolia commemorates Genghis Khan.

Peter I of Russia

PETER THE GREAT (1672 – 1725)

As a young man, in 1695, Peter I led a force against the Ottoman Empire. He later toured Europe to win allies in Russia's fight against the Ottomans. From 1700 – 1721, Peter I led Russia's newly improved army and navy in a successful war against Sweden, the leading power in northern Europe. This, and other foreign conquests, greatly increased Russia's political importance and helped to expand its trade. Peter I went on to reform the government, start Russia's first newspaper and found schools, museums and art galleries. In 1703, he built the city of St Petersburg and made it his capital. By the time Peter I died in 1725, he had transformed Russia into a great European power.

The battle of Poltava in 1709 was Peter the Great's decisive blow against the powerful Swedes.

ABRAHAM LINCOLN (1809 – 1865)

The 16th President of the USA, Abraham Lincoln is considered one of the greatest presidents. After working as a lawyer, he was elected to Congress in 1846. In 1856, he started campaigning for the newly formed Republican Party and began to gain attention for his strong anti-slavery views. In 1860, he was elected president. The following year, 11 Southern, pro-slavery states broke away from the Union to form their own Confederacy, triggering the American Civil War. As commander in chief, Lincoln steered the Union forces to victory. In 1863, he also announced the abolition of slavery throughout the USA. The Civil War ended in April 1865, when the Confederate troops surrendered. Five days later, Lincoln was shot by an assassin in Washington, and died the next day.

Lincoln is famous for saving the United States union.

VLADIMIR ILYICH LENIN (1870 – 1924)

The founder of the Communist Party in Russia, Lenin studied law but became involved in politics and a follower of Karl Marx. In 1903, he became leader of the Bolsheviks. At that time, Russia was ruled by a royal family. Conditions for ordinary people were very hard, and unrest began to grow. In 1917, rioting broke out. With World War I raging, life for most Russian people had gone from bad to

Lenin

worse. Lenin returned from exile and called for the government to be overthrown. In November 1917, the Bolsheviks attacked St Petersburg and seized power. Lenin became head of the new Communist government and moved the capital to Moscow. After Lenin's death in 1924, his body was preserved and put on public display in Red Square, Moscow.

FRANKLIN D. ROOSEVELT (1882 – 1945)

Roosevelt was the 32nd President of the USA, and the only person to be elected four times. His political career began when he was elected to the New York State Senate in

Roosevelt signs the USA's declaration of war against Germany.

1910. He later served twice as Governor of New York and, in 1932, received the party's presidential nomination. The following year, he beat Herbert Hoover to become president. Roosevelt led his country brilliantly through two of the greatest crises of the 20th century. He came to office at the time of the Great Depression, when the USA was suffering mass unemployment and a collapse of its economy. In response, Roosevelt introduced the New Deal, a programme of financial support and job creation. Roosevelt's third term in office was dominated by the USA's entry into World War II.

FDR on the American dime

MIKHAIL GORBACHEV (BORN 1931)

After studying law, Mikhail Gorbachev joined the Soviet Communist Party and quickly rose through its ranks. In 1985, he became party head and, five years later, was elected president of the USSR. As Soviet leader, Gorbachev gained worldwide fame for his programme of far-reaching political and economic reforms. He called these reforms perestroika (restructuring). Under these reforms, the power of the ruling Communist Party was reduced and there was a new openness (called glasnost). Following the USSR's example, other countries in Eastern Europe also called for an end to Communist rule. Gorbachev worked with the USA to reduce the threat of nuclear war and, in 1990, won the Nobel Peace Prize. In 1991, most of the Soviet republics broke away and formed the Commonwealth of Independent States. Gorbachev resigned as president and the USSR ceased to exist.

Mikhail Gorbachev with Ronald Regan in the 1980s

OSAMA BIN LADEN (BORN ca 1957)

Osama Bin Laden is the leader of Al-Qaeda, an Islamic terrorist organisation, based in Afghanistan but with links to other extremist Muslim groups around the world. Born into a wealthy Saudi Arabian family, Bin Laden left in 1979 to fight against the Soviet occupation of Afghanistan. He founded Al-Qaeda in the late 1980s. In 1990, Iraq invaded Kuwait and US troops were sent into the region – a move that Bin Laden fiercely opposed. In 1998, he was believed to have been behind the bombing of the US embassies in Kenya and Tanzania. Then, in September 2001, he masterminded the terrorist attack on the World Trade Center in New York, which left some 3,000 people dead. The USA declared a 'war on terror' and demanded Bin Laden's surrender. Despite the search continuing, however, Bin Laden has still not been found.

Bin Laden is believed to be hiding somewhere in the mountains on the border of Afghanistan and Pakistan.

Timeline of Leaders

		Leader	Leadership
ANCIENT	259–210 BC	EMPEROR QIN	Ruler of the Qin Dynasty and first emperor of China.
	100–44 BC	JULIUS CAESAR	Roman general who won civil war and became dictator of Roman Republic.
MEDIEVAL/MODERN ERAS	1162–1227	GENGHIS KHAN	Ruler of Mongolia; led Mongol armies in conquests of Central Asia.
	1533–1603	ELIZABETH I	Queen of England (1558–1603); led England to victory against the Spanish Armada.
	1672–1725	PETER THE GREAT	Ruler of Russia (1682–1725); led Russia in wars against the Ottoman Empire and Sweden; built city of St Petersburg.
	1732–99	GEORGE WASHINGTON	Leader of Americans during the American War of Independence; first President of the United States.
	1769–1821	NAPOLEON BONAPARTE	French general who took control of France on two occasions and became Emperor of France.
	1809–65	ABRAHAM LINCOLN	President of the United States of America (1860–1865); leader of Union in American Civil War; assassinated in 1865.
20TH CENTURY–	1870–1924	VLADIMIR ILYICH LENIN	Founder of the Communist Party in Russia; leader of the Bolsheviks during the Russian Revolution; a head of Russian government.
	1878–1953	JOSEPH STALIN	Leading figure in the Russian Revolution; General Secretary of the Communist Party; leader of Soviet Union in World War II.
	1882–1945	FRANKLIN D. ROOSEVELT	President of the United States of America (1933–1945); won four presidential elections.
	1889–1945	ADOLF HITLER	Leader of German Nazi party and leader of Germany in World War II.
	1893–1976	MAO ZEDONG	Leader of Chinese Communist Party, the Long March and Chairman of the People's Republic of China (1949–76).
	1869–1948	MOHANDAS GANDHI	Leader of non-violent protests for civil rights for Indians and the independence of India from British.
	1929–68	MARTIN LUTHER KING	Leader of civil rights movement in USA; assassinated in 1968.
	Born 1931	MIKHAIL GORBACHEV	Head of Soviet Communist Party and president of Soviet Union (1990–91).
	Born 1928	NELSON MANDELA	Leader of African National Congress in South Africa; president of South Africa (1994–99).
	Born 1957	OSAMA BIN LADEN	Leader of Islamic terrorist organisation Al-Qaeda.

Consequences

Ordered building of the Great Wall of China; unified China into a great power.

Unified the Roman Republic, reformed Roman laws, devised the Julian calendar.

Unified the Mongol tribes and built the huge Mongol empire.

Turned England into a mostly Protestant country; encouraged exploration and trade which led to beginnings of the British Empire.

Saved Russia from foreign invaders; transformed Russia into leading nation in northern Europe.

Helped to form the United States from a collection of British colonies into an independent nation.

Saved the French Republic from royalists; introduced the Napoleonic Code.

Led Union to victory against the Confederates in the American Civil War; brought slavery to an end in the USA.

Led the Russian Revolution that overthrew the Russian monarchy.

Transformed Soviet Union into powerful nation; millions killed in Great Purge of political enemies.

Led the Americans out of the Great Depression of the early 1930s; led the United States to victory in World War II.

Expanded Germany by invading other nations; ordered mass murder of Jews.

Founded the People's Republic of China; some policies disastrous for Chinese.

Improved lives of Indians and helped to make India an independent nation in 1947.

Gained better civil rights and voting rights for black Americans.

Introduced political and economic reforms to the Soviet Union; brought an end to communist rule in Soviet Union.

Despite 27 years in prison, helped to rid South Africa of apartheid and established democracy.

Catalyst for the USA's 'war on terror'.

Glossary

apartheid   system of laws in South Africa that divided black and white people from each other and took civil rights from black people

civil war   a conflict between two opposing groups in the same country

Cold War   a tense stand-off between the Soviet Union, and the USA and countries of western Europe, which began after World War II and ended in the 1980s

communism   political system in which the people own all of a country's property and all work for each other

empire   a collection of countries or lands ruled by one country

legion   a body of Roman soldiers about 5,000 strong

monarchy   a country's king or queen and family

province   part of a country that is ruled by another country

racial segregation   where people of different races are forced to live in different areas

republic   a country that is headed by a president who is elected by the people

royalists   people who support a king or queen.

Senate   the governing body of ancient Rome, which was made up of leading Roman figures

Index